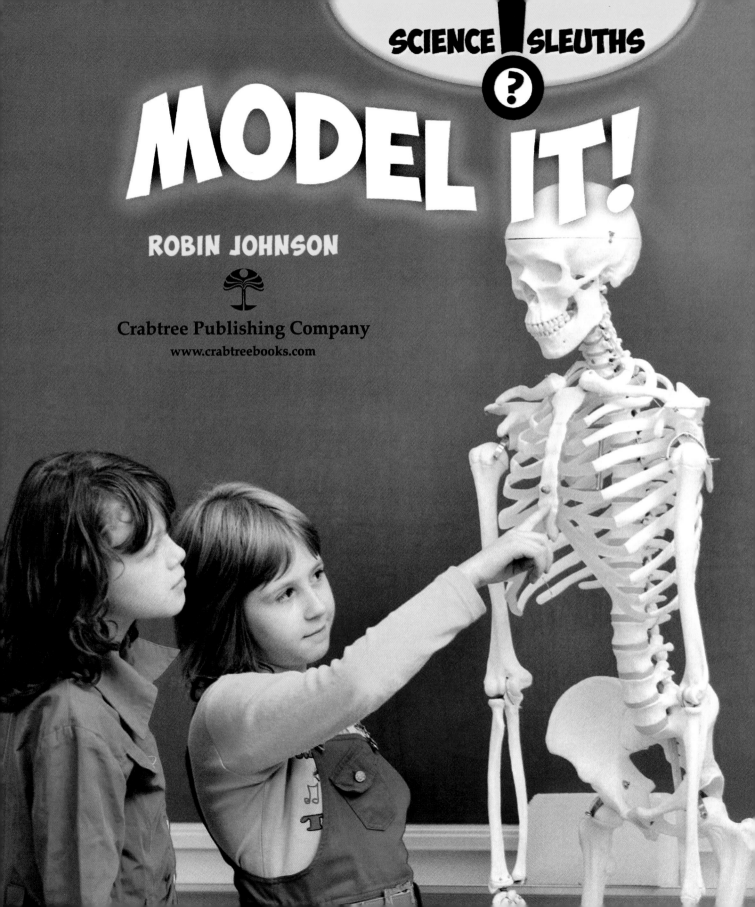

SCIENCE SLEUTHS

MODEL IT!

ROBIN JOHNSON

Crabtree Publishing Company

www.crabtreebooks.com

SCIENCE ! SLEUTHS

?

Author
Robin Johnson

Publishing plan research and development
Reagan Miller

Editor
Crystal Sikkens

Proofreader and indexer
Kathy Middleton

Photo research
Samara Parent

Design
Samara Parent

Print and production coordinator
Margaret Amy Salter

Prepress Technician
Tammy McGarr

Illustrations
Robert MacGregor p. 7 (top right);
Katherine Berti p. 15 & 16 (fox); Bonna Rouse p. 15 & 16 (plant);
Margaret Amy Salter p. 15 & 16 (sun and rabbit)

Photographs
iStock: Front Cover; Table of Contents; p. 6 (bottom); p. 8 (right);
p. 10 (left); p. 13
Shutterstock: © LehaKoK p. 22
Superstock: p. 21
Thinkstock: p. 4; p. 7 (middle right); p. 8 (left); p. 14
Wikimedia Commons: p. 20

All other images by Shutterstock

Library and Archives Canada Cataloguing in Publication

Johnson, Robin (Robin R.), author
    Model it! / Robin Johnson.

(Science sleuths)
Includes index.
Issued in print and electronic formats.
ISBN 978-0-7787-1541-2 (bound).--ISBN 978-0-7787-1545-0 (pbk.).--
ISBN 978-1-4271-1593-5 (pdf).--ISBN 978-1-4271-1589-8 (html)

    1. Simulation methods--Juvenile literature. 2. Models and
modelmaking--Juvenile literature. 3. Science--Methodology--
Juvenile literature. I. Title.

Q175.2.J63 2015   j507.2   C2015-901526-X
                                                C2015-901527-8

Library of Congress Cataloging-in-Publication Data

Johnson, Robin (Robin R.), author.
    Model it! / Robin Johnson.
        pages cm. -- (Science sleuths)
    Includes index.
  ISBN 978-0-7787-1541-2 (reinforced library binding : alk. paper) --
ISBN 978-0-7787-1545-0 (pbk. : alk. paper) --
ISBN 978-1-4271-1593-5 (electronic pdf : alk. paper) --
ISBN 978-1-4271-1589-8 (electronic html : alk. paper)
1. Scientific apparatus and instruments--Juvenile literature. 2. Science--
Methodology--Juvenile literature. 3. Scientists--Juvenile literature. I. Title.

Q185.3.J64 2015
502.8--dc23
                                2015008983

Crabtree Publishing Company

www.crabtreebooks.com   1-800-387-7650

Printed in the U.S.A./062015/CJ20150512

Published in Canada
Crabtree Publishing
616 Welland Ave.
St. Catharines, Ontario
L2M 5V6

Published in the United States
Crabtree Publishing
PMB 59051
350 Fifth Avenue, 59th Floor
New York, New York 10118

Published in the United Kingdom
Crabtree Publishing
Maritime House
Basin Road North, Hove
BN41 1WR

Published in Australia
Crabtree Publishing
3 Charles Street
Coburg North
VIC 3058

CONTENTS

HARD TO OBSERVE

Have you ever wondered how we learned so much about other planets—even though no human has ever been to them? The answer is science. Science is the study of the **natural world**. The natural world is made up of all living things, such as people, animals, and plants, as well as nonliving things, such as air, water, and rocks.

The natural world includes things we cannot see such as germs, as well as things that are far away such as the Moon.

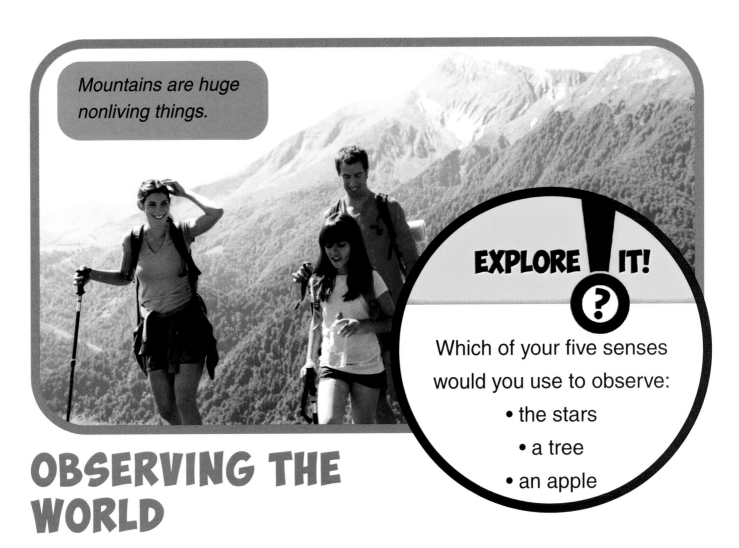

Mountains are huge nonliving things.

EXPLORE IT!

?

Which of your five senses would you use to observe:
- the stars
- a tree
- an apple

OBSERVING THE WORLD

Scientists are people who study the natural world to learn how and why things happen the way they do. They can **observe** things using their five senses: sight, hearing, touch, taste, and smell. But some things are hard to observe using just their senses. To study something that is hard to observe, a scientist will make a **model** of it. A model is an object that helps show how another thing looks or works.

SCIENTISTS USE MODELS

What do you think of when you hear the word "model"? You might think of a model airplane or car. Playing with these models helps you learn about the real things. Scientists use models to learn about things, too. They use models to **represent** parts of the natural world to help them answer questions and explain ideas.

There are no living dinosaurs anymore, but you can make models of them to learn more about them.

DIFFERENT KINDS

There are many different kinds of models. Some are **physical** models. This kind of model takes up space and has a form you can touch. Other models are **two-dimensional**, or flat. Maps, pictures, diagrams, and graphs are two-dimensional models. Scientists also make models on the computer. These kinds of models look like they take up space, but they are actually flat.

computer generated model

physical model

world map

EXPLORE IT!

?

These models all show Earth. How might each one help scientists study our world in a different way?

WHY USE MODELS?

Scientists use models to study things that are too hard to observe or cannot be observed directly. Things that are dangerous or are too big, too small, or too far away may need to be studied using models. Scientists might also use models to study things that lived long ago or which may take too long to observe.

Models help scientists study huge, faraway planets.

Volcanoes are mountains that shoot out hot, liquid rock from deep inside Earth. Scientists can use models to safely study how volcanoes work.

PUTTING MODELS TO GOOD USE

A model is more than a toy or an art project. Scientists use models to answer questions, explain how or why something happens, or **predict** what might happen in the future. To predict means to make your best guess what might take place next. A model is much easier to use and change than the real thing.

Scientists who study weather use computer models to predict the path a storm will travel.

THE SAME AND DIFFERENT

Every model is like the real thing in some ways. It is also different in some ways. For example, molecules are tiny pieces of material that make up everything around us. They are too small to see with just our eyes. Scientists use models of molecules to show how they join together to form different things.

This model shows a water molecule. The model is much bigger than the real thing and is made of different materials.

NIGHT AND DAY

Scientists also use models to show ideas that are hard to explain. For example, a scientist might use a model of Earth, called a globe, to explain how the rotation of Earth creates night and day.

ACT LIKE A SCIENTIST

Create this model with a friend. Use a sticker to mark where you live on a globe. Have your friend shine a flashlight on the sticker. The flashlight is the Sun and is shining daylight on the place where you live. Slowly spin the globe. Soon the daylight will be shining on another part of Earth and the place where you live will be dark.

EXPLORE IT!

?

How is this model the same as the real thing? How is it different?

STUDYING SYSTEMS

Scientists use models to study **systems**. A system is a group of parts that work together to do a job. Each part in a system is important. It has its own name and does its own job. Each part also affects the other parts. A good example of this is the human body. The human body is a system made up of many parts. Your brain tells your lungs to breathe and your heart to beat. These parts are all protected by your bones. Your skin covers and protects all the parts inside your body.

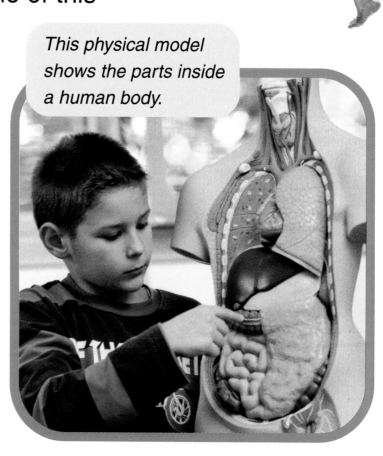

This physical model shows the parts inside a human body.

These students are learning how all the bones in our body are connected.

OUR DIFFERENT PARTS

We can use models to learn about the human body. Some models show where the parts inside our body are found. Other models show how our bones are joined together. Some models even teach us how to brush our teeth!

EXPLORE IT!

?

What would happen if the bone in your arm that connects your shoulder to your elbow was missing?

SYSTEMS IN NATURE

An **ecosystem** is a system in the natural world. It is made up of all the living and nonliving things in an area. Each part of an ecosystem has a job. Plants are called **producers** because they make their own food. Animals are called **consumers** because they eat plants or other animals. Earthworms, tiny living things called bacteria, and fungi, such as mold, help break down dead plants and animals and return **nutrients** to the soil. These things are called **decomposers**.

Plants are producers.

Animals are consumers.

Fungi, such as mushrooms, are decomposers.

FOOD CHAINS

All living things in an ecosystem need **energy**. Energy is the power to move and do work. A **food chain** is a model that shows the way energy moves from the Sun to plants, and then to animals. The arrows in the food chain diagram below show which way the energy is flowing.

1) Plants need sunlight, water, and nutrients from the soil to make food.
2) Animals eat plants and take in their energy.
3) Some animals hunt other animals for food. They take in the energy from the animal they eat.

15

MODELS HELP PREDICT

Scientists can use models to predict what will happen in a system. By following the flow of energy in a food chain, scientists can predict what will happen to an ecosystem if parts of the food chain change or are removed. For example, if all the plants in an ecosystem were removed, then the consumers would die because they would no longer be able to receive the Sun's energy by eating plants.

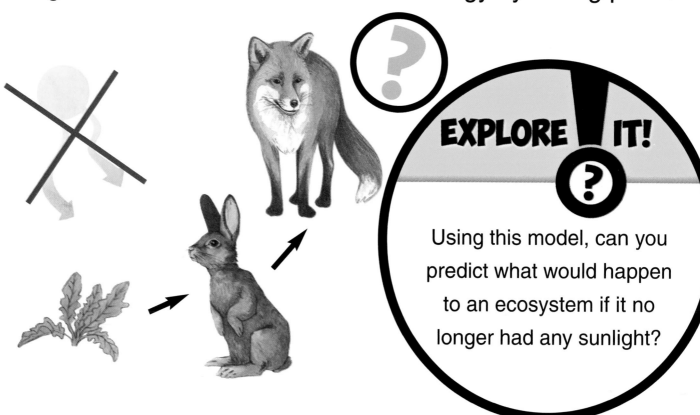

EXPLORE IT!

Using this model, can you predict what would happen to an ecosystem if it no longer had any sunlight?

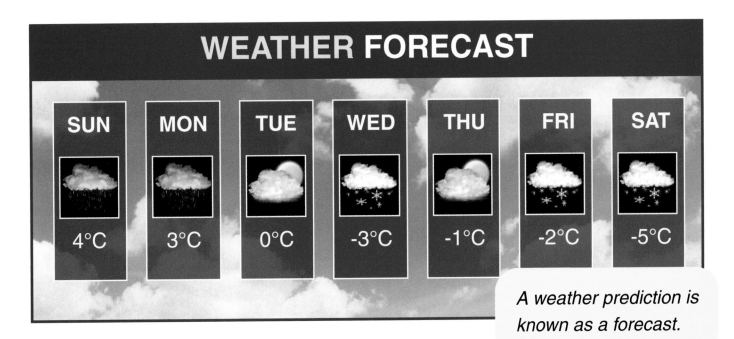

WEATHER FORECAST

SUN	MON	TUE	WED	THU	FRI	SAT
4°C	3°C	0°C	-3°C	-1°C	-2°C	-5°C

A weather prediction is known as a forecast.

WEATHER PREDICTIONS

Some scientists use computer models to help make predictions about weather systems. They base their predictions on what they know and what they observe, such as the air, water, **temperature**, and other parts of weather. Some parts of weather act together in certain ways. For example, water freezes at 0°C. If the temperature is above this, then water falls from clouds as rain. If the temperature is below this, then water falls as snow.

CHANGING MODELS

Scientists make models to learn more about things that are hard to observe. The more like the real thing a model is, the more useful it is. But scientists are always discovering new things. When they learn new information, they must change their models to show the new facts.

Until 2006, scientists thought Pluto was a planet that was part of our solar system. New information shows this is not true. Because of this discovery, models of the solar system had to be changed to include only eight planets, instead of nine.

MAP MODEL

Aiden's teacher asked the class to each make a map that showed all the states in the United States of America. Aiden made a computer model that showed 48 states. After doing some research, he found out Alaska and Hawaii are also part of the United States, even though they are far away.

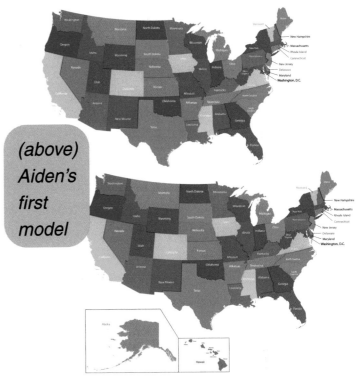

(above) Aiden's first model

Aiden changed his computer model so it included Alaska and Hawaii.

EXPLORE IT!

?

Imagine that scientists learned Earth has two moons instead of one. Would they need to change the model to the right? Why? Describe how the new model might look.

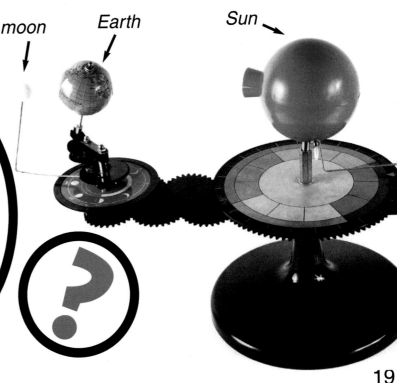

moon *Earth* *Sun*

MAKE A DIORAMA!

Now it is time to act like a scientist and make a model! A **diorama** is a physical model that shows a scene from the world. Some dioramas are the same size as the real things, and others are much smaller. Follow the steps on the next page to make a small diorama of an ecosystem.

This large diorama shows the home of prairie dogs.

1. Get an empty shoe box.

2. Paint or color the inside of the box. Draw sky, land, and other parts of the natural world.

3. Hang the Sun from the top of the box. The Sun warms Earth and lets plants make food.

4. Add some models of living things. Use toy animals or make your own. Include plenty of plants for animals to eat.

5. Add some nonliving things. Plants and animals need water to drink. They also need rocks for shelter.

6. Label the parts of your ecosystem. Turn back to page 15 for help.

OBSERVE THE WORLD

Use your diorama to learn more about dinosaurs and the natural world. Observe how living things need all the parts of the ecosystem to survive. What would happen if you took something out of your diorama? Predict how it would affect the entire ecosystem. Could this be what caused the dinosaurs to die?

Act like a scientist and find out more about these animals that lived long ago.

LEARNING MORE

BOOKS

Engineers Build Models by Reagan Miller. Crabtree Publishing Company, 2014.

Looking at Maps and Globes by Rebecca Olien. Scholastic, 2012.

How Muscles and Bones Hold You Up: A Book About Models by Marcia S. Freeman. Rourke Educational Media, 2007.

WEBSITES

Build model volcanoes, mummies, roller coasters, and more at this fun website.
http://discoverykids.com/games/

Learn how to make a model hand, a fossil, and lots of other cool projects at this website.
www.sciencekids.co.nz/projects.html

Visit this site to learn about plants, animals, weather, energy, and much more!
http://easyscienceforkids.com/

GLOSSARY

Note: Some boldfaced words are defined where they appear in the text.

consumer (kuhn-SOO-mer) noun
A living thing that must consume,
or eat, food to survive

decomposer (dee-kuhm-POH-zer) noun
A living thing that breaks down dead
plants and animals

food chain (food cheyn) noun A model
that shows how energy passes from one
living thing to another

nutrient (NOO-tree-uhnt) noun
A substance that living things need
to grow and stay healthy

observe (uhb-ZURV) verb To look
at something carefully to learn more
about it

physical (FIZ-i-kuhl) adjective In a form
you can see and touch

predict (pri-DIKT) verb To use what you
know to guess what might happen

producer (pruh-DOO-ser) noun
A living thing that produces, or makes,
its own food

represent (rep-ri-ZENT) verb To stand
for or act in place of

scientist (SAHY-uhn-tist) noun A person
who studies the natural world

system (SIS-tuhm) noun A group of
parts that work together as a whole

temperature (TEHM-per-a-chur) noun
How warm or cold the air is

two-dimensional (TOO-di-MEN-shuh-nl)
adjective Flat; not taking up space

*A noun is a person, place, or thing.
A verb is an action word that tells you
what someone or something does.
An adjective is a word that describes
what something is like.*

INDEX